Along the Coast
Cullen to Pennan

GW00632238

Capstan and lighthouse, Cullen Harbour. (Portknockie in the distance).

Along the Coast
Cullen to Pennan

By
Stanley Bruce

Published by
BARD BOOKS
on behalf of the
Banffshire Maritime & Heritage Association

Photography by
Stanley Bruce

Second Edition.

ISBN 978-1-907234-08-8.

Reprinted in 2011 by Bard Books.

on behalf of the Banffshire Maritime & Heritage Association.

All proceeds from the sale of this book will go to the Banffshire Maritime Heritage Association.

(The 1st Edition was published in 2007).

Printed by McKenzie Quality Print, Dyce, Aberdeen.

Lobster creels at Gardenstown Harbour.

Contents

Macduff War Memorial.

Portsoy War Memorial.

*Finial of Cullen
Mercat Cross.*

Banff Harbour Marina – The 'Heritage Haven'.

Introduction - The aim of this book is that you can use it when travelling by car (Or walking) and see the popular sites, and the interesting places that you would probably pass without seeing or realising they were even there.

The impressive coastline on the Moray Firth between Cullen and Pennan has recently been the focus of several tourism initiatives, including the redevelopment of Banff Harbour to a marina. The harbour has now been deepened to allow access at most tides and new floating pontoons with power outlets and lighting have been installed in both of the inner basins.

The town of Macduff still has its shipyard, which is actively competing in the world market and retains skills in wooden and steel shipbuilding. Funds were provided for an upgrade of the harbour slip to make it safer and capable of taking much larger boats, this work was completed early in 2009.

Sea trips are now regularly available from both Banff and Macduff, and are becoming more and more popular with tourists, particularly those interested in dolphins, whales, and birdlife.

Another wonderful and becoming more known tourist attraction is 'Troup Head', which is ten mile east of Macduff. This is now a RSPB Nature Reserve. Troup Head in the summer months is a haven for seabirds and currently hosts a colony of around 1300 breeding pairs of gannets; this is currently the only breeding gannet colony on the mainland of Scotland. Gannets are not the only seabirds to be found here, there is an abundance of life particularly in the summer months - puffins, guillemots, cormorants, fulmars and many other types of seagulls can be seen. RSPB have plans to develop this site; a visitor centre and pathways are amongst their development plans.

Of course, this coastline has all the features you could possibly want from the seaside; and we will travel along it from the Bow Fiddle Rock west of Cullen heading eastwards through its charming villages and towns to the wonderful secluded village of Pennan.

I am very happy to state that this is the second edition of this book, the first edition was A4 in size, however, this edition has been reduced to A5 so it is easier to carry with you, and it has more pages. This edition, has been updated, has better directions, a lot more detail, and additional photographs. The whole book has been re-written and reformatted; I hope you enjoy it.

Stanley A. Bruce, BSc; I.Eng, I.MarEng, MIMarEST.
Chairman – Banffshire Maritime & Heritage Association.

*Make your way to Portknockie and follow the signs for the **Bow Fiddle Rock**.*

The Bow Fiddle Rock - The Bow Fiddle Rock is an amazing natural rock sculpture, which can be seen from Cullen, but is best viewed from the village of Portknockie, a little west of Cullen.

The Bow Fiddle Rock viewed from Portknockie.

*From the Bow Fiddle Rock take a ten-minute walk east along the headland past a small wooden fulmar sculpture and down the path to the beach, and on the way down the path you will pass on your left another natural arch known as the **'Whales Moo'**.*

The 'Whales Moo'. (The Whales Mouth).

Wooden Fulmar Sculpture.

*Follow the path as it drops down to the beach a little further east and you will come to a sacred fresh water spring known as **Jenny's Well**.*

Jenny's Well.

*A little further, heading east, you will come to a large cave, which is known as the **Preacher's Cave**.*

The Preacher's Cave (St. Duane's Den) – This cave was given this name because after 1843 it was used by the 'Free Church' following its break away from the Church of Scotland. A local elderly man said he remembered a minister still preaching here as late as the 1930's.

The Preacher's Cave (St. Duane's Den).

*From here, back track to your car, and from the Bow Fiddle Rock drive west and take the first road on the left (Admiralty Street), at the T-junction at the top of this road, turn right, then turn left, and left again at the next T-junction. Follow this road to a T-junction joining the A98. Turn left, and approximately ½ mile on the right is the **Cullen Bay Hotel**.*

Cullen Bay Hotel – The hotel stands on the site of the former Farskane (Farskin) House, which was owned by the Gordon family and dates back to at least to 1677. In 1924, the house (Or at least part of it) was converted by Mrs Simpson of Cullen to the Cullen Bay Hotel. Tel No. 01542 840432. *You can walk along the railway viaduct, by crossing the main road (A98), if you wish.*

Elizabeth Hamilton, armorial panel 1677 Ex Farskane House.

Cullen Bay Hotel, Cullen.

*Turn right out of the Cullen Bay Hotel car park (Taking care for traffic coming around the bend), and head down the hill, take the next road on the left under the former railway viaduct to the beach car park and **Cullen Golf Club**.*

Cullen Golf Club – The club was founded in 1870, initially with nine holes designed by Old Tom Morris (1821 to 1908). In 1907, it was extended to eighteen holes to the design of golf professional Charlie Neaves. Tel No. 01542 840685.

*Due west of the clubhouse are three rocks known locally as the **Three Kings**.*

The Three Kings – Three large prominent rocks stretching out to the sea adjacent to the clubhouse of Cullen Golf Club.
There are public toilet facilities adjacent to the southern most rock.

Cullen Golf Course and the prominent rocks known as 'The Three Kings'.

*From the car park return to the main road (A98), and turn left into Cullen. Drive up the hill, and under the Railway Bridge and park in the square. There is parking on the left and toilet facilities, and parking on the right behind **Cullen's Mercat Cross**.*

Cullen Mercat Cross – St. Mary is the patron saint of Cullen, and the Mercat Cross has a carving of the Virgin and Child. The cross, which was erected 1675 to 1696 originally stood near ***Cullen Old Kirk.*** However, it was re-erected on Castle Hill in the 1820's, when the village was moved from aside Cullen House to where it is today. In 1872, it was re-erected in The Square. Category B listed.

Virgin and Child, Mercat Cross, Cullen.

Mercat Cross.

*Across the street is the **Cullen War Memorial and Millennium Garden**.*

Cullen War Memorial and Millennium Garden -
The Countess of Seafield laid the foundation stone for the war memorial 6th August 1920. It was designed by John Wittet of Elgin. The memorial commemorates the dead 'Officers and men of Cullen and district' from WW1 and WW2. Category B listed.
To celebrate the millennium, a garden was established adjacent to the memorial.

Cullen War Memorial.

Cullen - Famous for a local soup made with smoked fish, potato and onion affectionately named 'Cullen Skink', which is enjoyed regularly by the locals, is a must have for every visitor and can be found in the cafés in the square. The seatown of Cullen prospered during the herring boom of the 19th century and the harbour was greatly developed around 1817. Tourist Information is located in The Square near the toilets, which are adjacent to the war memorial. A nice carving of the Seafield arms adorns the tourist information building.

*If you fancy a walk along the viaduct, it is best accessed from the bottom of North Deskford Street. Drive up the hill (Grant Street) heading west from behind the **Mercat Cross**, and take the second road on the right, park just around the corner in North Deskford Street, a small path from the bottom of the road leads you to the top of the **Cullen Railway Viaduct**.*

Cullen Railway Viaduct – This huge structure was built in 1885 at great expense, but is now redundant and has been adapted into a walkway and cycle route. From the top of this amazing structure, great views of Cullen and the Moray Firth are to be had. A cycle route marker, one of one thousand sponsored by The Royal Bank of Scotland and the National Lottery proudly stands atop of the viaduct. From here, you have a fine view of the harbour, and if you are lucky, you may see some dolphins or a Minke whale in the bay.

About 100 yards from the path there is an embankment, due south of this is 'Castle Hill', and at the top of the hill is a crudely built stone structure with four ancient armorial panels built into it, and an unusual seat made of stone.

Clamber up the hill if you are interested.

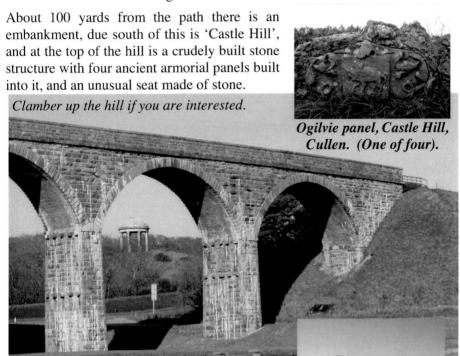

Ogilvie panel, Castle Hill, Cullen. (One of four).

Cullen Railway Viaduct and Pomona.

At the west end of the village is a fine-looking circular Pomona known as the 'Temple of Fame', it was designed by James Playfair (1755 to 1794) in 1788, however, it was not built until 1822 by William Robertson (1786 to 1841) of Elgin. It used to house a statue of Mercury blowing a trumpet, but sadly, it has not since WW2. The golden sand of Cullen Beach is complimented with three large rocks known as the **Three Kings**. These stand aside the **Cullen** *Cycle route marker, Cullen Viaduct.* **Golf Course**, and of course, the Banffshire Coast is renowned for golf and the fantastic courses at **Duff House Royal** in Banff and **Royal Tarlair** in Macduff are both a delight to practitioners of the game.

We will now drive back up the hill, going straight ahead at the crossroads into South Deskford Street, at the T-junction veer to the right into Cathay Terrace, *then take the next road on the right (Old Church Road) and follow this road until you come to a car park, park here and walk to **Cullen Old Kirk.***

Cullen Old Kirk - The old village of Cullen was established around 1189 and the first known church dedicated to St. Mary was founded here in 1236. On the 26th October 1327, Elizabeth de Burgh (b.1289) wife of King Robert the Bruce died at Cullen Castle. Her entrails were removed during the embalming process, and buried in the church; her body was taken south and buried in Dunfermline Abbey. Inside is an impressive carved stone monument to Alexander Ogilvie (d.1554), which has a recumbent knight inside an elaborate canopy.

Cullen Old Kirk.

| *Alexander Ogilvie.* | *James Ogilvie.* | *James Ogilvie.* |
| *(d.1554).* | *(d.1509/10).* | *(d.1505).* |

Ogilvie coats of arms at Cullen Old Kirk.

Cullen Old Kirk has several coats of arms, and several table type gravestones, many with symbols of mortality.

Over the cemetery wall, you can see the rear of Cullen House.

<u>**Cullen House**</u> – A large privately owned turreted mansion house on the western outskirts of Cullen now split into flats. The house existed originally in 1600 as an L plan castle, however the house has been extended many times in the 17th, 18th, and 19th centuries. Originally, the town of Cullen stood adjacent to the house; however, it was moved to its present location in 1822. Category A listed.

Coat of Arms, Cullen Old Kirk. Dated 1603.

Postcard of Cullen House taken from the west. (Balfour, Cullen).

Cullen House is over-looked by a large prominent hill to the west known as the 'Bin o' Cullen' it stands 320m (1050 feet) high. (See page 18 for a photograph).

*Back track along Old Church Road, turning left back down Cathay Terrace, and follow the road into Seafield Place (Past the Seafield Estate building), to the T-junction of Seafield Street (A98). Turn right (Up hill) and follow the A98 eastwards, 2 miles east take a left turn where it is sign-posted **Findlater Castle**, follow the signs up to a car park adjacent to a farm steading.*

Findlater 'Bee-hive style' Doo-cot. (Dove cot / Pigeon house).

<u>**Findlater Castle**</u> – From the car park adjacent to the former farm buildings take the path heading north. On the left, you will see a well-preserved 16th century doo-cot. Findlater Castle stands on a remote fifty-foot high promontory at the shore. The name Findlater is derived from Norse 'Fyn' meaning white and 'Leitr' meaning cliff, so named because of the white quartz stone in the rock. The castle as seen today was built in 1455 by the Ogilvie's of Deskford on the site of an earlier castle dating from at least the 13th century, which is thought to have been built on the site of an even earlier Danish (Viking) fort. The castle was Abandoned by the Ogilvie Earls of Findlater in 1600 in favour of **Cullen House**. (See page 15). To the west of the castle, is a wonderful but scarcely walked on beach, known as 'Sunnyside Beach'.

Findlater Castle.

16

*From the farm car park drive to the bottom of the farm road and turn left, make your way eastward to the village of **Sandend**. At the T-junction as you enter the village, turn left and park in the car park immediately on the right.*

<u>Sandend</u> - With its quaint little harbour (*A little further ahead north*), and its wonderful yet in the winter scarcely walked-on beach, which stretches about half a mile eastwards, Sandend is popular with caravan owners and walkers. The village dates back to at least 1624, the kirk session records of this date refer to the fishermen of Sandend being rebuked for baiting their lines on a Sunday. The harbour was built in 1883, and probably incorporates earlier work. Most of the houses were built by fishermen in the early 1800's. No 56 Sandend was formerly the village school.

The harbour is category C(S) listed by Historic Scotland and many of the fishing cottages are either category B or C(S) listed. The harbour is currently independently owned by Sandend Harbour Trust Company.

Sandend Harbour.

Sandend Harbour.

From the north end of the car park, there is a path, which takes you directly to the beach. The beach still has a row of concrete blocks, which were placed here during WW2, and at the east end, there is still two large pillboxes.

Sandend Beach with the Bin o' Cullen (1050 feet high) in the distance.

WW2 Pill boxes and coastal defences, Sandend Beach.

Leave Sandend by heading south through the village, this road takes you back to the A98, at the T-junction turn left. About 1/3 mile on the left is the ***Glenglassaugh Distillery***.

Glenglassaugh Distillery – The first distillery at Glenglassaugh was built in 1875 and continued in production until 1907, however it continued in malt production until 1922. The distillery we see today was built in 1960. In 1986, it also closed, but remained in use as a bonded warehouse. In 2008, it reopened, and today is supposed to be open to visitors. Due west of the distillery is an old windmill minus the blades, it is known locally due to its shape as the 'Cup and Saucer', and is category A listed by Historic Scotland.

The 'Cup and Saucer' windmill (Glenglassaugh Distillery behind).

*From Glenglassaugh Distillery take a left turn back onto the A98, and drive 2 miles to **Portsoy**. Enter the village and park on Seafield Street, near the Station Hotel.*

In the main through fare (Seafield Street) is the War Memorial, a great ice-cream shop, and a wonderful bookshop 'Bookends', which has many rare books and is well worth a look. Adjacent to the Station Hotel is Loch Soy, which is used as a boating pond during the summer.
At the east end of Seafield Street are public toilet facilities.

*From here, take a left turn at the toilets, which is sign posted for the Salmon Bothy, and follow Church Street north to **Portsoy Harbour**.*

Portsoy Harbour – The harbour consists of two parts, the old and the new. The old part was first built in 1692-3 by Sir Patrick Ogilvie (d.1714) the 8th Laird of Boyne and lies to the west. The newer harbour of 1825-8 built by Colonel F. W. Grant on behalf of his brother Sir Lewis Ogilvie-Grant (1767 to 1840) the 5th Earl of Seafield lies to the east. Both of these harbours host the 'Scottish Traditional Boat Festival', which is now an annual event, and attracts tens of thousands of visitors over one weekend in July.

Scottish Traditional Boat Festival, Portsoy Old Harbour

Portsoy was once famous for marble, most notable being its use in the fireplaces in the Palace of Versailles built by King Louis XIV of France; however at Portsoy Harbour there is a marble shop where you can buy a piece for yourself. *Opposite the Shore Inn are public toilet facilities.*

The Marble Shop, Portsoy Old Harbour. (Former Corf House).

*Follow the road along the harbour and shoreline east, past Barclays lorry depot, until you come to the car park of the **Portsoy Salmon Bothy**.*

Portsoy Salmon Bothy – The Bothy, which was built in 1834, was in 2008 restored to its former glory, and is now used as a small museum of salmon fishing, a venue for talks and musical entertainment, and for family history research. Tel 01261 842951.

Portsoy Salmon Bothy.

*From the Bothy follow the road along the coast past the caravan site and over a small bridge to a car park. The row of derelict buildings due south, are a former sail-works, and farmhouse. From here, you can follow the coastal walks eastward. Looking west you can see a large earth mound in the cemetery. On the south side of the mound is **St. Colm's Well**.*

St. Colm's Well - St. Colm's Well, Portsoy is thought to have been built around the 6th century, and is one of Portsoy's hidden treasures. It is one of two Banffshire wells dedicated to St. Colm, who came to the northeast with St. Columba in the sixth century.

At the east cemetery gates, there is a path heading east, where you can walk along the banks of the 'Soy Burn' (Stream), and then over a bridge and up the hill for some fine views of Portsoy.

St. Colm's Well, Portsoy.

Portsoy Caravan Site.

*Drive up the hill (St. Combs Road), and take a left (Institute Street), and left back onto Church Street. At the T-junction turn left, back onto the A98 (Seafield Street), and take the next road on the left before the outskirts of the village, follow this road for 1.5 miles crossing a small narrow bridge at Scotsmill. You can walk to **Boyne Castle** from here, however you will need to walk along the road up the hill for about 100 yards and climb over a gate into a field, the castle is at the other end of the field over another gate, hidden in the trees.*

Boyne Castle - Hidden away in the trees above the 'Burn of Boyne' is Boyne Castle (East of the burn) and its doo-cot (West of the burn). The castle was built c1580 by Sir Alexander Ogilvie (b.1539), but today it stands as a ruin. Craig o' Boyne, an earlier castle once stood at the Moray Firth coast near where the quarry stands (Site of the Lime Works). Boyne is typical of many neglected castles in the northeast, and it is clear that if Boyne Castle and others in a similar condition are not saved soon they will be lost forever. **If visiting, please be aware of the dangerous condition of the castle.**

Boyne Castle.

Sign at Boyne Castle.

Boyne Castle Doo-cot.

*From Scotsmill, follow the road up the hill and turn right, follow this road for 1 mile to the T-junction of the A98 and turn left. Travel for 2 miles, and on the right there is a lay-by with the **Banff Strike Wing Memorial**.*

Banff Strike Wing Memorial – RAF, Norwegian, Canadian, Australian, and New Zealand crews flew sorties from Banff Aerodrome during World War II. Flying Mosquito and Beaufighter planes they attacked German convoys sailing down the west coast of Norway. Each day a scout plane with Norwegian crew scanned the Norwegian coastline for German ships, and reported their locations back to the other crews. It was then their mission to fly over and destroy as many of the German ships as possible. An interesting DVD can be purchased at the Boyndie Visitor Centre, or in Chapter and Verse Bookshop in Banff.

Banff Strike Wing Memorial on the A98 (Erected in 1989).

*Looking inland from the memorial, you can see the **Boyndie Wind Farm**.*

Boyndie Wind Farm - Seven turbines were erected in 2006. The windmills stand on the former site of the Boyndie Aerodrome, which closed at the end of WW2. An eighth turbine was added in 2009. The aerodrome is used by the Grampian Cart Club on selected Sundays.

Sunset at Boyndie Wind Farm.

*Follow the A98 heading east for 1.5 miles, and take a left turn at the signpost for the **Boyndie Visitor Centre.***

The Old School Boyndie Visitor Centre – The Old School Boyndie Visitor Centre was established in the redundant Victorian school buildings at Boyndie. It has been awarded a four star visitor attraction status. In the centre is a nice café, a shop and display area, and a display relating to RAF Banff. In the grounds, there is a pond and some short, but nice walks.

From the Visitor Centre take a left turn and follow this single-track road for ½ a mile to the T-junction of the

Pond at the Boyndie Visitor Centre.

*B9139. Turn right, and at the crossroads, which is about 500m ahead, turn left, this road takes you to the village of **Whitehills**, at the entrance to the village is the Parish War Memorial, and straight ahead takes you to **Whitehills Harbour**. (For toilet facilities turn first right after the Post Office into Loch Street, the toilets are immediately on the left behind the bus shelter).*

Whitehills Harbour - This village was once predominately a fishing port, and even had its own lifeboat station from 1922 to 1969 (Now converted to a house). In 2001, the harbour was converted to a marina, which is very popular and it is usually packed with yachts. Adjacent to the harbour is a nice **Compass Rose,** which was built into the ground in 2001.

Compass Rose Whitehills.

If you happen to visit here in the evening as the sun sets, you may be lucky enough to see a spectacular sunset. (See the rear cover of this book).

Sunset at Whitehills Harbour.

Whitehills Marina.

For more history of Whitehills, see our publication 'Whitehills Through the Years'. ISBN 978-1-907234-04-0.

Whitehills Lighthouse.

From Whitehills Harbour, follow the road eastwards along the shore and you will come to a great play-park for the kids with toilet facilities situated aside **Blackpots Harbour.**

Blackpots Harbour – This very small harbour was formerly used by salmon fishermen and by the Blackpots clay factory, which stood where the caravan site now stands. The Salmon Bothy was converted to the caravan site shop. The factory made red-clay items such as drainage pipes, & roofing tiles using clay from Knock Head.

Keep heading east along the single-track road, and admire the views across Boyndie Bay to Banff and beyond. ½ a mile along this road is **The Red Well.**

The Red Well - A chalybeate well thought to have been built in Roman times, stands near to the shore, it is said to be protected by the ghost of an old woman. In olden times, the well would have had a keeper; and she may well be the ghost. Another strange phenomenon regarding the well is that during the sunrise on the morning of the summer equinox (Twice a year) a ray of light enters the well and lights up the inside when the outside is still in darkness.

__The Keeper o' the Well.__

She guards the well,
Night and day,
And you, she will repel,
If you cause an affray.

The Red Well (Now re-pointed and has a gate fitted).

*Follow the road up the hill past the well, and turn left at the T-junction onto the B9038. Follow the road for approximately ½ mile and turn left at the staggered crossroads sign-posted Inverboyndie. On your right is **Inverboyndie Kirk**. There is no car park at the kirk, and you will have to park further ahead and walk back if you wish to visit.*

Inverboyndie Kirk – This church dedicated to St. Brandon, was built in 1634. A battle between Danish Vikings and the Scots led by King Kenneth III was fought here c1000, and the Scots defeated the invading Vikings. This battle is remembered with the names Arrdanes (Danes with arrows) west of the Boyndie Burn, and Swordanes (Danes with swords) east of the Boyndie Burn. In a field across the road from Inverboyndie Kirk, approximately 30 yards north is said to be where the dead Vikings were buried in a large pit.

Ancient gravestone,
Inverboyndie Kirkyard.

*Return to the road and head eastwards, over a small bridge over the Boyndie Burn, and take the second road on the left to car park at **Banff Links**.*

Banff Links - The beach at Banff Links with its golden sands, its great play-park, and its large caravan site is very popular with tourists. There is a nice walk west along the coast to the **Red Well** and **Whitehills**, and another eastward to **Banff** via the harbour. The beach is also popular with surfers who surf with 'Xtreme Scotland'. www.surfandwatersportsclub-scotland.com

Banff Links with Whitehills and Knock Head in the background.

Play-park at Banff Links.

*Drive back out of the car park and turn left, follow this road to the T-junction of the A98, and turn left, follow this road for ½ a mile into **Banff**.*

Surfing at Banff Links.

Banff - The historic and royal burgh of Banff is well known for its 17th, 18th, and 19th century architecture, the most prestigious being *Duff House,* which is now chiefly used as an art gallery. The category A listed harbour, has been converted to a marina, and at the heart of Banff is the historic *St. Mary's Old Kirkyard.*

At the T-junction of the A98 (Bottom of Seafield Street) turn left and park, then walk back to Banff War Memorial.

Banff War Memorial – 27th May 1921 Princess Louise (1867 to 1931) HRH Princess Royal and wife of the Alexander Duff (*1849* to *1912*) 1st Duke of Fife laid the foundation stone of the Banff War Memorial in Castle Street. The memorial was designed by Dr. William Kelly of Aberdeen, and is made of grey Aberdeen granite. The memorial commemorates 143 dead of WW1 and 39 dead of WW2 (36 men and 3 women). The memorial was unveiled in 1922. Category B listed.

Banff War Memorial.

Next to the War Memorial is Banff Castle.

Banff Castle – The castle in Banff as seen today was built as a mansion house for James Ogilvie (1714 to 1770) 3rd Lord Deskford of Cullen in 1750, to the design of John Adam. It was built on the site of a much earlier castle, possibly dating back to the 12th century. Part of the castles mediaeval walls and moat remain, and can be seen at the north of the castle. Archbishop James Sharp (1618 to 1679) was born here. Since 1950, it has been owned by Banff Castle Community Association, and is available for functions.

Banff Castle. Tel 01261 815325.

Captain George Duff Memorial – Situated in the grounds of Banff Castle overlooking Banff Bay is a memorial to Captain George Duff who fought at Trafalgar in 1805. He was married to local lass Sophia Dirom. The memorial was funded by the Banff Rotary Club, Banff Preservation Society and the Friends of Duff House and was erected on the 21st October 2005, the 200th anniversary of his death. At the battle of Trafalgar, George captained the 74 gun ship 'Mars', but he had a ghastly death when a cannon ball blew his head off. George was the son of Banff Sheriff Clerk James Duff, and George's son midshipman Norwich Duff (1792 to 1862) aged thirteen, was also at Trafalgar, he however continued his naval service and later became a Vice-Admiral. A monument to George Duff stands in the crypt of St. Paul's Cathedral, London, adjoining the tomb of Nelson.

Garden of Remembrance and Well.

Captain George Duff Memorial, Banff Castle.

*From here, you can if you wish walk southward to the shops on Banff's High Street. However, we will now leave Banff Castle and turn right, heading north, follow the road to the bottom of the hill and turn sharp right and park in the car park, which is just a short walk from **Banff Harbour Marina**.*

Banff Harbour Marina – The harbour dates from 1625, when it was known as 'Guthrie's Haven'. Prior to the harbour being built the water behind a large sand bank (Shingle bar) at the mouth of the River Deveron referred to as the 'Bar Lake' was used as a natural harbour. This shingle bar was removed during WW2 and used to build Boyndie Aerodrome. From 1770-5, John Smeaton (1724 to 1792) made major improvements to Banff Harbour; and from 1775-80 he built Banff Bridge. Smeaton was famous in Great Britain for other projects such as the Eddystone Lighthouse. From 1818-28 Thomas Telford (1757 to 1834) built the Lighthouse Quay, it took so long to build due to a storm in October 1819, which caused a considerable damage to the works. Category A listed by Historic Scotland.

Banff Harbour Marina.

*From Banff Harbour, continue heading along the coast, and park your car in the small car park located a little bit before **St. Mary's Old Kirkyard**.*

St. Mary's Old Kirkyard – In 1471, St. Mary's Kirk was re-built, perhaps replacing a Carmelite Chapel, which is thought to have stood on or near this site. It was a large kirk for its time measuring approximately 94' long x 25' wide. It is said that this relatively small cemetery contains approximately 40,000 bodies. There are several symbols of mortality and coats of arms on the older gravestones in the Kirkyard.

Robert Sharp coat of arms.

Gateway to St. Mary's Old Kirkyard.

Coat of arms, Carmelite Street dated 1675.

Old houses, No's 1 to 5 High Shore, Banff.

*From the gateway of St. Mary's, walk past the old house with the corbelled tower (Shown above) and in front of you on your left is the **Plainstones**.*

Plainstones, Banff – The Plainstones on Low Street are a raised area of flagstones. Here we have the ***Mercat Cross,*** which dates from c1550. Two carvings of Banff's emblem the 'Virgin and Child', one dated 1628 and another so badly eroded we cannot tell its date, presumably it is older, perhaps from c1550. These two carved stones may have once been part of the Mercat Cross. Built into the wall is the colourful coat of arms of King Charles I, dated 1634. Also located here is an old cannon said to have been brought back from Sebastopol in Russia after the Crimean War.

Virgin and Child Effigy (1628).

16ᵗʰ century Mercat Cross.

Charles I Royal coat of arms (1634).

Sebastopol Cannon.

*On the opposite side of the road is the former **Tolbooth Hotel.***

The Tolbooth Hotel – This building was built in 1801 on the site where the original Tolbooth once stood. James Macpherson the Freebooter in 1700 was locked up in the Tolbooth before being hanged. The clock in Banff was reputedly put forward one hour to ensure he was hanged because a reprieve was on its way. He may have been hanged here at the ***Mercat Cross,*** on the Gallowhill, or perhaps on the hill where the Sandyhill doo-cot is located, the location is disputed.

*In front of the former Tolbooth Hotel is the **Biggar Fountain.***

Biggar Fountain - The Biggar Fountain, an ornate Victorian Gothic drinking fountain was erected in Low Street in 1878. It was designed by architect John Rhind of Edinburgh. It is nineteen feet high and made of Binny freestone. The inscription reads 'Presented to the town of Banff in memory of Walter Biggar Esq., and Mrs. Ann Duff, his wife'. Walter Biggar is recognised as being the man who established links to sell herring with the Baltic countries. The fountain was gifted by the Rev. Dr. and Mrs Blaikie relatives of the Biggar's. It is said that they were inspired to make the gift after reading the life of Banff Naturalist Thomas Edward (1814-1886)

Biggar Fountain, Low St, Banff.

who had stated that it would be an advantage to the town to have a memorial sited on the old site of the ***Mercat Cross***. It was restored in 1995, and is category B listed by Historic Scotland.

Near the fountain is Chapter and Verse Bookshop, which sells many local books, & maps including many of the Banffshire Maritime & Heritage Association. (See inside the rear cover of this book for details).

*From here drive (Or walk) south along Low Street, past the Sherriff Court and on the right is St. Mary's Car Park. Situated aside the car park is the Collie Lodge, now used as the **Banff Tourist Information**.*

Banff Tourist Information – It is located in the Collie Lodge, which was built in 1836, and was originally a gate lodge to Duff House, which had an entranceway here prior to the car park and bypass being built in 1960. The lodge is category B listed by Historic Scotland. *Public toilets are located behind the lodge. Tel 01261 812419.*

Banff Tourist Information - Collie Lodge.

*Adjacent to Banff Tourist Information is **Banff Parish Church.***

Banff Parish Church – This fine church dedicated to St. Mary was built in 1790 and can seat 1200 people. It was originally built without a steeple; however, a steeple was erected in 1849. The church is a notable landmark particularly at night when it is beautifully lit.

Banff Sea Tree – The 'Sea Tree' erected in 1992, proudly stands in St. Mary's Car Park. It was sponsored by Mobil North Sea Ltd., and designed by Frances Pelly. It bears the motto of the Macpherson clan 'Touch not the cat but a glove', a link to Macpherson the Freebooter who was hanged here in 1700. It has many other symbols carved on it, with one being incorrect, see if you can spot it.

Banff Sea Tree.

St. Mary's - Banff Parish Church.

*On the High Street, about 50 yards heading north from the entrance to St. Mary's Church is **Banff Museum**.*

Banff Museum – Banff Museum is located in the library building on the High Street. Its build was funded in 1902 by Scotsman Andrew Carnegie (The richest man in the world at the time). It is only open during the summer months, and its most interesting exhibit is a replica of the Deskford Carnyx, which is an extremely rare Pictish war trumpet. The history of Banff Museum goes back to 1828 when a group of local men founded Banff Institution for Science, Literature, and the Arts.

Deskford Carnyx replica. (Banff Museum).

A Pieta from the 15th century depicting the Virgin Mary holding the body of Christ was uncovered in *St. Mary's Old Kirkyard* in 1862. This extremely rare sculpture is the only known pieta ever found in Scotland. It is currently kept in Banff Museum. A mediaeval carved oak panel possibly depicting Coventina Goddess of Wells is another very interesting item. In the museum, you can find out all about Banff's most famous men - Thomas Edward the Naturalist, and James Ferguson the Astronomer. Tel 01771 622807.

Pieta. (Banff Museum).

Banff Museum and Library, High Street, Banff.

Carved oak panel possibly depicting Coventina Goddess of Wells. (Banff Museum).

*Exit St. Mary's Car Park by turning right, then turn left at the T-junction, then turn immediately right, and follow the single-track road past the entrance to Duff House Royal Golf Club to **Duff House**.*

Duff House – Duff House was designed by William Adam and built from 1735-1739 for William Duff (1697 to 1763) 1st Earl Fife. However, it was James Duff (1729 to 1809) 2nd Earl, who completed the interior in 1748-1759. Duff House Country House Gallery as it is now known today, hosts a wealth of paintings from the National Galleries of Scotland. It also has a shop and a café. The house did not always look as good as it looks today it has a chequered history; it has been a prisoner of war camp, a hotel, and a sanatorium, and was bombed in WW2. Tel 01261 818181.

Duff House. www.duffhouse.org.uk

*Heading south from Duff House, there is a very nice walk through **Wrack Woods**.*

Wrack Woods – The walk begins at the *Fife Gates*. Inside the gates you can either take the path on the left or follow the road, both take you to the *Ice House*. The path takes you past an interesting gravestone to three dogs, Bevis (d.1872), Tip (d.1873), and Barkis (d.1875) who were pets of the Earl Fife, and lived at Duff House.

Fife Gates – Gateway comprising of two polished ashlar octagonal gate-piers with moulded step caps supporting fine carved stone urns decorated with fruit and flowers, erected in the 18th century. The house adjacent to the gates was formerly Duff House Laundry.

Ice House – As the name implies this building was Duff House's refrigerator, it was packed with ice during the winter months and was used to store perishable goods such as meat and fish.

Fife Gates stone urn.

Ice House, Wrack Woods, Banff.

*Follow the path (20 mins approx) or the road (15 mins approx) from the Ice House to the **Duff Mausoleum**.*

Duff Mausoleum – This is quite an elaborate building built in 1790 by James Duff (1729 to 1809) 2nd Earl Fife, possibly on the site of a much earlier chapel of St. Mary founded by King Robert the Bruce. At the rear of the building is a fine tomb of Provost Alexander Douglas (d.1658) of Banff. Over the fence behind the mausoleum, below the path, and partly hidden by a fallen tree (The first large one lying $90°$ to the path after the fence) is a well dedicated to St. Mary.

Dog's gravestone, Bevis, Tip, and Barkis, Wrack Woods, Banff.

Duff Mausoleum, Wrack Woods, Banff.

Memorial to Provost Alexander Douglas, Wrack Woods.

St. Mary's Well, Wrack Woods, Banff.

From here if you wish you can follow the road and walk all the way to the Bridge of Alvah (About 2 miles), and onward to Macduff (About five miles).

*From Wrack Woods / Duff House make your way back to the main road passing **Duff House Royal Golf Club**.*

<u>**Duff House Royal Golf Club**</u> – The first golf course in Banff known as 'Banff Golf Club' was founded in 1871, and was located at ***Banff Links***. The course was moved to its present location in 1909-10 when Alexander Duff (1849 to 1912) 1st Duke of Fife donated the land. In 1923 to 1924, the course was redesigned, and on 1st Jan 1925 was renamed Duff House Royal Golf Club at the request of Princess Louise. www.theduffhouseroyalgolfclub.co.uk

Duff House Royal Golf Club. (Tel: 01261 812062).

*Return to the main road and turn right, heading for Macduff over **Banff Bridge.***

Banff Bridge - The seven-arch Banff Bridge over the Deveron was built in 1775-80 by John Smeaton (1724 to 1792) and its build costs were funded by Parliament. A date stone with 1778 and George III is located on the north side of the bridge above the central arch. Category A listed by Historic Scotland.

Banff Bridge and the River Deveron.

41

Often seen at the waters edge, near and sometimes under the bridge are several ducks and often swans, or if you are lucky a grey heron, an otter, or perhaps a Canada Goose.

Swan, grey heron, and duck in the Deveron River at Banff Bridge.

East of the bridge is Doune Hill, which in Gaelic means Castle Hill, presumably a castle or fort once stood at this location. Today a small temple known as the **Temple of Venus** *is the most noticeable landmark.*

A December sunrise behind the 'Hill of Doune'.

Further upstream on a small island adjacent to the east bank of the river, past the Macduff Distillery houses, which are visible from the bridge, is a ruined **Fishing Temple.**

Fishing Temple – This temple was built by William Duff *(1697 to 1763)* the 1st Earl Fife. The circular building has two stories, each one with a small room with a fireplace. The first floor is accessed by a double stairway made to a similar style to that of Duff House. The architect is thought to have been William Adam (1689 to 1748) who also built *Duff House* and the *Temple of Venus.* Currently the temple is roofless and the flooring on the first floor is gone. No windows or doors remain and the staircase is now in a **dangerous condition.** Access is by dodgy stepping-stones over a narrow stretch of water a little upstream from the distillery houses, which are only visible when the tide is out and the river is low.

Fishing Temple.

Visiting this is only recommended for the fit, and most adventurous of tourists. Category B listed. Grid Ref NJ691628.

Heading east cross Banff Bridge, turn left heading for Macduff, and take the next road on the right (Church Street), which takes you up the hill to **Macduff Parish Church.**

Macduff Parish Church - The striking parish church, which dominates the skyline, was built in 1805 originally with a large steeple. However, today it is seen with an Italianate cupola and clock, which was erected in 1865. The church has two stained glass windows to the memory of those who died in WW1, and a set of three windows dedicated to Elizabeth Mantell an African missionary nurse who lived part of her life in Macduff. The Bodie lair inside the east wall of the cemetery has some interesting memorials.

Macduff Cross – Adjacent to the church is the Town Cross, which was erected in 1783 when the village of 'Doune' at the request of James Duff (1729 to 1809) 2nd Earl Fife was created a royal burgh of barony by King George III and renamed Macduff. The shaft of the cross is said to have been made using remnants of an older cross, taken from Fife, thereby making a link between the ancient and modern bearers of the Fife name.

Macduff Anchor – Also adjacent to the church is a thirteen-foot long anchor, which was placed at this location in June 1972. The anchor was pulled up from the seabed by the net of local fishing boat BF3 'Golden Spinney', skippered by Maurice Slater of Macduff, and is believed to be from an 18th century sailing ship; it's thought to weigh around three tons.

Macduff Parish Church (2005).

Macduff Cross.

Anchor at Macduff.

*From the church, take the road up the hill (Shand Street), then right at the T-junction into Gellymill Street, follow this road (Gellymill Road), past the houses, until you come to Dounemount Care Home, park the car here, from here you can walk to the **Temple of Venus**.*

Temple of Venus – The Temple of Venus on the Hill o' Doune was built by William Duff (*1697* to *1763*) the 1st Earl Fife as a feature to improve the skyline. It was built to the design of architect William Adam (1689 to 1748) of Edinburgh. In the days of sail, it became a noted landmark for seafarers. It is said to have contained a statue of the Goddess Venus but today it stands empty. In the late 1930's prior to WW2 it was struck by lightning and badly damaged, however it was rebuilt after WW2. Category B listed. Grid Ref NJ698638.

Temple of Venus.

*Back track along Gellymill Road leading to Gellymill Street, then take the 2nd road on the right (Market Street), in front of you is the Knowes Hotel, and on your right is the **Macduff War Memorial**.*

Macduff War Memorial – The 70 feet high octagonal tower stands proudly on a hill known as 'Canker's Knowe'. It was built by two retired stonemasons, Alexander Brown (79) and Magnus Johnstone (68) they commenced the work April 1921 and finished in October 1922. It was their contribution to the war. (See photo page 5). It commemorates 150 men who died in WW1 and 51 men who died in WW2.

Macduff War Memorial Foundation Stone.

*Follow the road eastwards and at the T-junction of Duff Street, turn left down the hill to **Macduff Harbour**.*

Macduff Harbour - A fishing port for more than two centuries, Macduff is still home to many fishing boats, and to the Northeast's only remaining shipbuilders, Macduff Shipyards.

Macduff Harbour key dates:
East and West Harbours built 1770.
Lord Fife's breakwater built 1820 to 1830.
North Basin built 1878.
Lighthouse Quay Built 1903.
Slipway and Princess Royal Basin built 1921.
Fish Market built 1966.
Slip modernised 2008-9.

Guillemots.

Fishing off the Lighthouse Quay is a very popular activity with visitors and local lads, and around the harbour area, a wide variety of birds can be seen such as guillemots, cormorants, seagulls, and ducks, and occasionally a seal or even a dolphin.

For more information on Macduff, see our publication 'Macduff Through the Years' ISBN 978-09547960-8-2.

Fishing boat BF47 'Concorde' leaving a flat calm Macduff Harbour.

Banff to Stavanger Yacht Race - The 'Banff to Stavanger' annual yacht race was first sailed in 1984. The total distance was 280 nautical miles and the fastest crossing was thirty hours, which was set in 2003. The race was normally held in June and a variety of shore based activities usually organised to coincide with the race. In 2007, and 2008 it was known as the 'North Sea Yacht Race', sadly 2008 was the last race held.

Maritime Garden – Across the main through fare (Crook o' Ness Street) at the east end of the harbour, is a Maritime Garden, which has stones forming part of a compass set into the ground and the Bodie Fountain. The Bodie Fountain, which is made of granite, was gifted to the town in 1910 by local showman Walford Bodie (1869 to 1939), who lived in the Manor House in Skene Street, approximately 200 yards up the street from here. The fountain is dedicated to the memory of his daughter Jeannie who died in 1909 aged only eighteen. (This is the fourth site where this fountain has stood). Although the garden has tidied up what was an unsightly area, there is very little maritime about the garden.

Yachts in Macduff Harbour. (2006 Yacht Race).

Maritime Garden, Crook o' Ness Street, Macduff.

*Across the main road, where the harbour Café now stands, was the home of probably the most famous man who has ever lived in Macduff - **Peter Anson.***

Peter Anson (1889 to 1975) – Marine artist and writer he lived in Macduff for twenty years. He was born in Portsmouth, the son of Rear-Admiral Charles Anson. In 1910, at the age of twenty-one Peter became a monk. In 1921, Peter was a co-founder of the 'Apostleship of the Sea', an organisation dedicated to administering to the material and spiritual needs of Catholic seafarers.

Peter Anson.

Peter quit being a monk in 1924 at the age of thirty-five and began to write and paint professionally. In 1927, at the age of thirty-eight, he published his first book titled 'The pilgrim's guide to Franciscan Italy'. It was to be his first of forty-seven books published.

In 1936, he became a founder member of the *'Society of Marine Artists'* which became an official society in 1939. The society received the Royal Charter in 1966 and henceforth became *'The Royal Society of Marine Artists'*. In 1936, he briefly lived in Portsoy, before moving to Banff; in 1938 he moved to Macduff. Peter lived here in Macduff for nearly twenty years and in his later life (1969) he wrote, *'Life on Low Shore' described as 'Memories of twenty years among fisher folk at Macduff, Banffshire, 1938 - 1958'*. This book is one of his most popular and widely read books. During his time in Macduff, he had his own sailing boat called the 'Stella Maris' (Star of the sea), which was lost in 1952. In 1966, Pope Paul VI made Peter a 'Knight of the Order of St. Gregory'. In 1967, he became the first curator of the 'Scottish Fisheries Museum' in Anstruther, a post he held for only one year. In 1969, Peter retired to Caldey Island, his former island-home; there he kept himself busy drawing, painting, and writing. At Caldey, he enjoyed the rare status of a Reformed Cistercian choir-oblate. In 1974, due to failing health, he was compelled to seek a mainland home and he was accepted into the community of the Sancta Maria Abbey, Nunraw, East Lothian. Peter died in St. Raphael's Hospital, Edinburgh, 10 July 1975, and is buried at Nunraw Abbey. Four hundred of his maritime paintings were donated to the museum in Buckie.

A Buckie Fisherman's tribute to Peter (In Doric):

"Peter's the maist winnerfu' mannie ah ever met - well-kent in scores o' ports - a man wi' the sea in's bleed, a skeely drawer o' boats an' haibers an' fisher fowk, a vreeter o' buiks, a capital sailor, an' 'a chiel.... He's a byordinar mannie!"

Translated: 'Peter is the most wonderful man I've ever met – well known in scores of ports – a man with the sea in his blood, a skilful drawer of boats and harbours and fisher folk, a writer of books, a capital sailor and a young man.......He's an extraordinary man!'

For more on Peter see our book titled 'Back to the Sea'. ISBN 978-1-907234-00-2.

Photo of Peter's House, Harbour Head, 1944 to 1958.
(Now demolished – the Harbour Café is now located here).
Photo by Frank Ritchie.

Macduff Lighthouse, fishing nets, and floats.

From the harbour follow the harbour road past Macduff Shipyards, or follow the main through fare and take the road on the left opposite the Maritime Garden sign-posted **Marine Aquarium.**

<u>Macduff Marine Aquarium</u> – The aquarium is home to a great variety of fish and creatures from the Moray Firth. The aquarium has their own divers, who regularly enter the large open-air tank, the deepest in Scotland, and feed the fish, during which the catfish usually rise to the occasion. *Tel 01261 833369.* www.macduff-aquarium.org.uk

Macduff Marine Aquarium.

Large Pollock.

Starfish.

Sea Anemones.

Macduff Marine Aquarium.

*From Macduff Aquarium, follow the coast road east and approximately ½ mile ahead the road drops down a hill to **Tarlair**.*

Tarlair – East of Macduff you will find Tarlair an art deco lido built in the 1930's. In its heyday, this place was jam-packed with swimmers and boat-paddlers, and it is only just in recent years that the swings and slides have been removed. The pool officially closed in 1996; however, it is still used by model boat enthusiasts. It has recently been category A listed by Historic Scotland, and hopefully this listing will lead to some restoration being carried out. One idea is to convert the pool into a lobster hatchery. Adjacent to the pool is another natural sculpture known as the 'E'e o' the needle' (The eye of the needle). Cleaved Head, a promontory immediately east was once a Pict fort.

Also nearby is an old well house, which still stands, although in quite a poor condition. This well was popular in the days when people took the waters for medicinal purposes. The water stopped running through the well in WW2 when a mine was washed ashore, and blew up the Well Cottage. Sangs the lemonade manufacturer in Macduff are said to have found the source of the water and it is this water, which they say is used in their Macduff factory.

Tarlair Lido.

Crazy Frog and the well at Tarlair.

E'e o' the needle, (Eye of the needle) Tarlair, Macduff.

Sanderling.

Old postcard of the well and cottage at Tarlair.

*Head back up the hill and take the second road on the left, drive up the hill to the T-junction with Buchan Street (A98), turn left and adjacent to the lay-by on the left is **Royal Tarlair Golf Course**.*

Royal Tarlair Golf Course – The golf course overlooks Tarlair Lido, and has tremendous views of the Moray Firth, especially at the challenging thirteenth hole. www.royaltarlair.co.uk Tel 01261 832897.

Golfing at Royal Tarlair Golf Club.

From Royal Tarlair Golf Club we head east on the A98, and after 0.5mile take a left onto the B9031 where sign-posted for Gardenstown. After six miles, take a left turn down the single-track road sign-posted St. John's Churchyard.

St. John's Churchyard – This church is dedicated to St. John the Evangelist. In 1004AD, Vikings invaded here and a great battle took place known as the 'Battle of the Bloody Pits'. Legend tells us that St. John helped the Scots win the battle and he was rewarded with a church built here in his name in 1010. Built into the wall of the first church were three skulls of beheaded Danish Viking chiefs. Today we can see the roofless ruin of the church built in 1513. The unknown location of the 'Bloody Pits' somewhere nearby is where the slain were buried after the battle. From here, you have great views of **Gardenstown** and **Crovie**. Grid Ref NJ791645.

St. John's Churchyard.

Leave the car park at St. John's and back track to the A98, and then turn left. Follow the A98 for 1 mile and turn left where sign-posted Gardenstown.

If you want to see the Parish War Memorial take a right turn, ½ mile before the Gardenstown turn-off, where sign-posted Gamrie Churchyard.

Gardenstown – Gardenstown was founded in 1720 by Peter Garden, and was built predominantly as a fishing village. The houses of the seatown follow the line of the shore and other houses cling to the steep hillside above Gamrie Bay.

*When you enter the village turn left, heading downhill, keep going down until you come to several garages, then turn left to **Gardenstown Harbour**.*

Gardenstown Harbour - The harbour was built in 1720 and later rebuilt in 1868. It is usually crammed with both small fishing boats and pleasure craft. To the east, there is a very nice coastal walk to the wonderful village of *Crovie* and to the west a nice beach and a walk to *St. John's Churchyard*. *At the harbour, there is a heritage centre and public toilet facilities.*

Gardenstown Harbour.

*Back track up the hill, and immediately before the Spar shop, veer to the left, follow this road for ½ mile, and turn left where sign-posted for **Crovie**. Follow this single-track road, and park in the car park / viewpoint on the left. Here you will see a sculpture called '**Scottish Athena**', and have some great views of **Crovie**. Walk down to the village, and stroll along its single street eastward, or follow the path westward past the 'SS Vigilant' cairn to **Gardenstown**.*

Crovie - The small village of Crovie (Pronounced Crivie) with its single street and no road was once home to many fishermen, but today the houses are mainly owned as holiday homes. Its single pier has been in the news, due to it crumbling away due to severe winter seas. This to my mind is a very special place, and there is nowhere else I would rather be on a beautiful summer's day.

Crovie from the viewpoint.

Twelve feet high 'Scottish Athena' sculpture, Crovie, created by Rosie Bradshaw from ash wood, erected in 1990.

Crovie. (Looking east).

Cairn erected to commemorate the bravery of the men and women from Gamrie Parish who rescued the crew of the SS 'Vigilant', 11th February 1906. (Erected in 2006 by the Crovie Preservation Society).

Back track to the main road and turn left, when you reach Bracoden School veer to the left, follow this road to Northfield Farm, drive through the farm and follow the dirt track road down to a car park. Park here and walk approximately ½ mile to **RSPB Troup Head.**

RSPB Troup Head - East of Crovie the 450 feet high cliffs of Troup Head are usually packed with breeding seabirds during the summer months. The site is now owned by the RSPB.

Gannets
Fulmars
Puffins
Guillemots
Great Skuas
Kittiwakes
Shags
Cormorants
Seagulls
Razorbills

Great Skua.

Gannet.

Herring Gull.

Cormorant.

Puffins and Guillemot. (M. Bragg).

*Back track through the farm and after approx 1 mile take the next road on the left, this road takes you to a T-junction with the B9031, turn left and drive for a little over 1 mile and turn left where signposted **Cullykhan Bay / Fort Fiddes**.*

Cullykhan and Fort Fiddes – The beautiful secluded beach of Cullykhan is often deserted, and you can have it all to yourself. The adjacent promontory was once home to a Pict settlement and a later fortification built in the 18th century known as 'Fort Fiddes'. Also in view from the top of the promontory looking west is 'Hells Lum', a large opening (Cave) in the cliffs, which looks like it is smoking when seas are rough.

Cullykhan Beach.

*Back track to the main road and turn left, follow this road for just under 1 mile, and turn left where signposted for **Pennan**.*

Pennan - Our journeys end for this book is the village of Pennan. Once famous for its mill stones is nowadays more famous for its association with the 1983 film 'Local Hero'. The red phone box featured in the film is the most dialled into phone box in the whole of Scotland. Fishermen used to land their catch in the small harbour, but like the other small fishing villages in the Northeast when the larger steam drifter fishing boat was introduced the fishermen re-located to the larger harbours such as Fraserburgh and Macduff. In its secluded setting with its quaint harbour and pebble beach Pennan is very popular with tourists. It is so tempting just to sit at the beach listening to the rumble of the pebbles as they roll in and out with each wave, you could say tranquillity was born here.

Pennan.

The red phone box at Pennan.

The coastline of the county of Banff originally stretched from Portgordon a little west of Buckie to Cullykhan Beach a little west of Pennan. However, on the 16th May 1975 the county of Banff ceased and was split between Aberdeenshire and Moray, with the county border lying a little east of Cullen. The coastline today between Cullen and Pennan, as marketed today, is a place for families, couples, artists, photographers, and bird-watchers; in fact, it has something for nearly everyone.

Many of the photographs included in this book are taken from one of my slideshows titled 'The Great North East Corner – The coastline - Cullen to Collieston' and can be found on www.electricscotland.com the largest Scottish website in the world with more than 170,000 pages.

For more information on the coastline between Cullen and Pennan, and to see some more of my photographs see:

www.banffshiremaritime.org.uk Our Association website.
www.webhistorian.co.uk   Visit the Banffshire Maritime section.
www.world66.com   Photos of the Northeast from Elgin to Aberdeen.
www.banffharbour.co.uk   Photos of Banff Harbour.
www.banff-macduff.com   A variety of photos around Banff and Macduff.
www.bbaf-arts.org.uk   A selection of photos taken around Aberdeenshire.
www.discovergardenstown.co.uk   Photos of Gardenstown.
www.heraldry-scotland.co.uk   Heraldic panels around the Northeast.
www.banffshirecoast.com   Lots of information on the coast.

Map

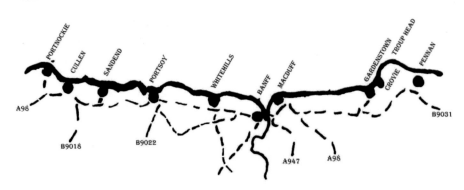

The coastline Cullen to Pennan.
(Not to scale).

Scotland's Treasure
Living at the Banffshire Coast,
To me it is a pleasure,
What beauty she does boast,
She truly is, 'Scotland's Treasure'.